EBERHARD HAVEKOST

GUEST

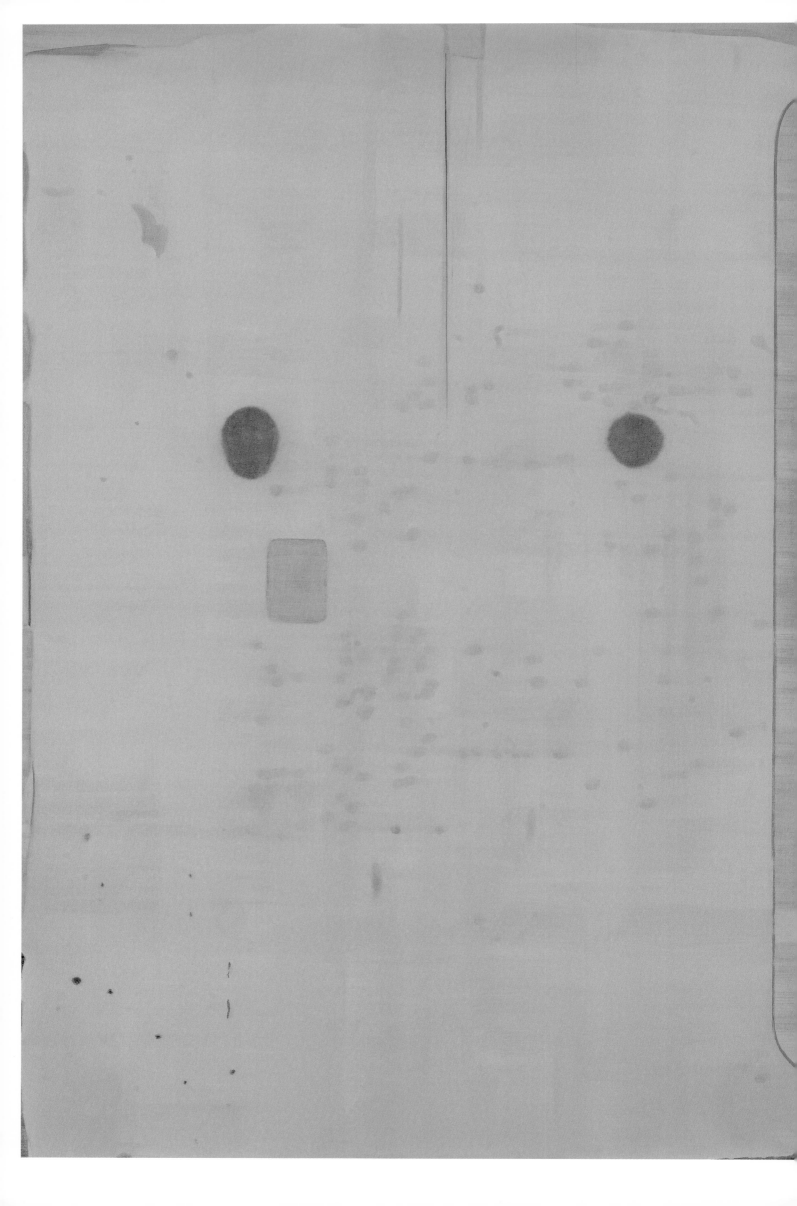

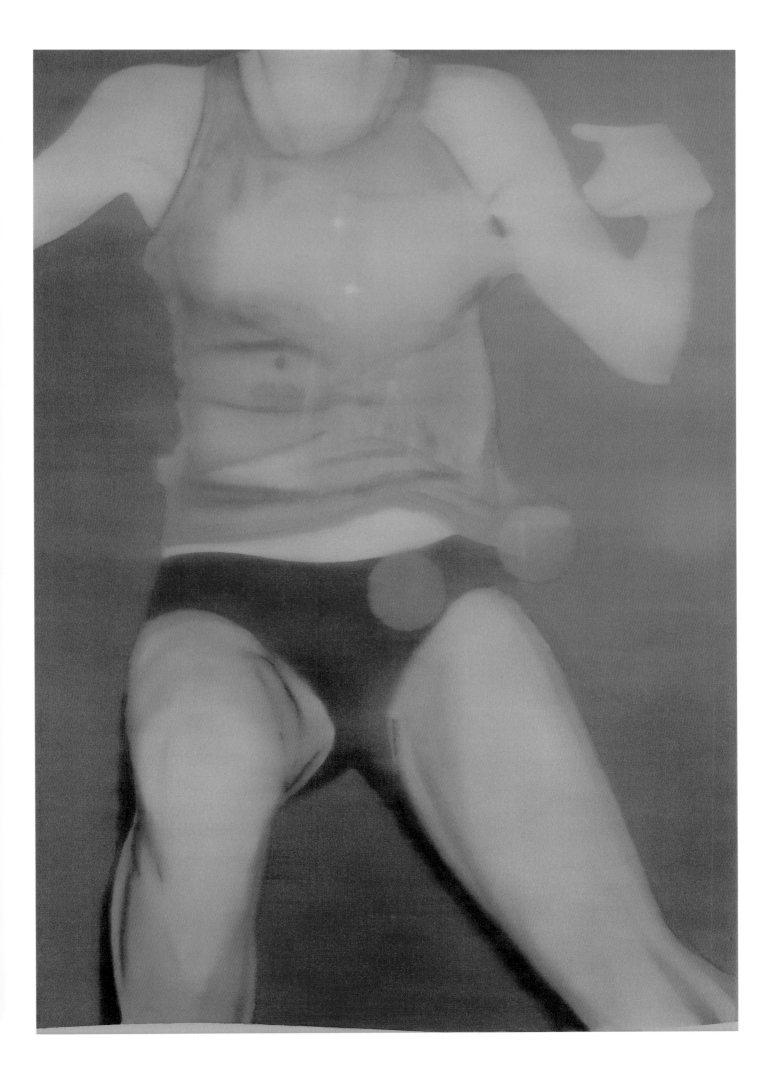

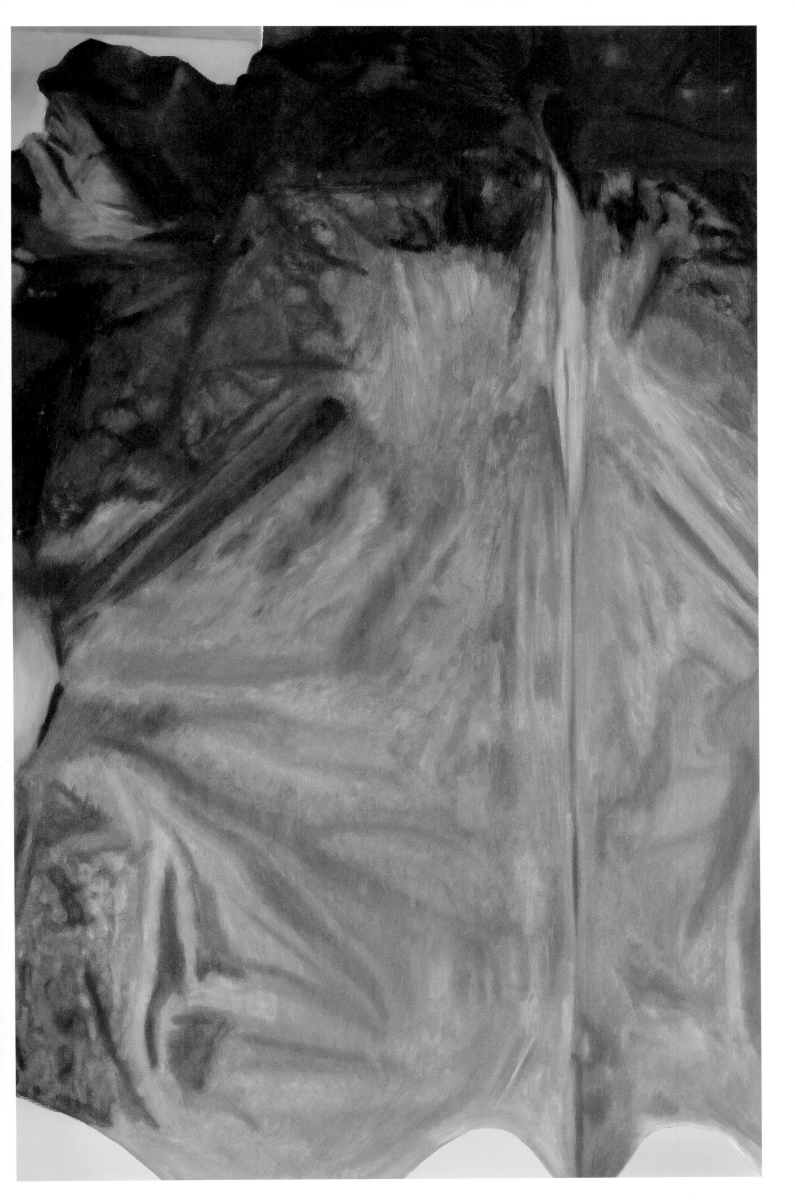

John Constable, *Study of the Trunk of an Elm Tree* (c.1821)
© Victoria and Albert Museum, London

WEEPING NOOTKA AND THE FLASH

CRAIG BURNETT

Caspar David Friedrich, *Winter Landscape* (c.1811)
© The National Gallery, London

A tree, spooky in its pendulous limbs, emerges from the gloom. Ribbons of murky green uncurl and hang like flesh from a zombie. Patches of purple, turquoise and orange interrupt the dominant set of hues, and everything is cast in a ghoulish pall. While instantly recognizable as a depiction of a tree, the scale and attitude of this painting conjure thoughts of other things: the rotten remains of a shipwreck, perhaps, or a huge candelabra oozing with wax. Stepping back you see another tree—the same tree—caught in the same spectral light. The greens are richer; the branches droop in different directions. Beside this tree there are others—one with branches outspread like a dancer's arms; another of swampier greens, limbs filling the picture plane; yet another, framed by a deep lake of black—until, finally, nine trees engulf the viewer's field of vision. The overall mood is dark and eerie, yet the trees have a forceful, pulsating presence.

The origins of Eberhard Havekost's *Gast 1–9* (2010), lie somewhere outside a hotel in Germany, where the artist decided to photograph a tree, stumbling in the dark, shooting it in fugacious bursts of flash, illuminating each tree in a beat, before it became night once more. Selecting nine of the resulting photographs, and ordering them in a visual rhythm, Havekost then set about painting a series of works on a scale large enough to make the viewer feel engulfed by a forest. The species of the tree is, if my identification is correct, a Weeping Nootka False Cypress, or Yellow Cypress, or Alaska Cypress (among other regional names), an evergreen native to the west coast of North America, but now common in urban spaces all over the world because landscapers like its hardiness and decorative qualities. These details are worth mentioning only insofar as they demonstrate that both the location and the type of tree, while knowable, are largely unimportant, although it is difficult to resist the evocativeness of the name. There is nothing remarkable about this particular tree: it is, like so many of Havekost's paintings, a depiction of an overlooked element in our urban landscape.

Yet trees almost always connote something beyond the everyday fact of their existence. Ever since Eve sampled the forbidden fruit, and probably before, the tree has been one of western culture's most overworked motifs. Artists have freighted it with ideas about mortality or immortality, knowledge, the sovereign individual, time, symmetry, beauty, wisdom and the resilience or vulnerability of nature. In fact, the tree has provided the perfect structure on which artists and poets, philosophers and semioticians, can hang the beliefs of an era, using it as a metaphor to explore human consciousness and linguistic systems.

In the middle ages, for instance, forests were considered to be full of demons and best eradicated, whereas today their destruction usually symbolizes everything that is calamitous about modernity. When the eighteenth-century idealist philosopher George Berkeley wanted to illustrate his theory that 'to be is to be perceived'—that reality exists only in the mind—he posed the question whether a tree really falls in the forest if there is no one there to perceive it. In 'The Oaks', an early work by the Romantic poet Friedrich Hölderlin, the speaker encounters a grove of trees and declares: 'Each one of you is a world, you live as the stars in heaven/each one a god, bound together in freedom.'[1] A variation of this arch-Romantic, almost pantheistic, view of nature transcendent is visible in the paintings of Hölderlin's contemporary, Caspar David Friedrich. The trees depicted in his *Winter Landscape* (1811) play an intermediary role between heaven and earth: a man has dropped his crutches and thrown himself against a rock, hands clasped together in prayer beneath some evergreens that cradle a crucifix. In the background, the silhouette of a cathedral echoes the shape of the foreground trees, both pointing to heaven. It is impossible to ignore the allegorical import of the trees and the religious power they embody: Friedrich's trees sustain salvation and point to a better place. A decade or so later, John Constable painted *Study of the Trunk of an Elm Tree* (c.1821): a work so fastidiously observed and touched by delicate emotion—though apparently bereft of the spiritual significance of Friedrich's painting—that it could be considered a portrait. The sinewy Cypresses near Arles that Vincent van Gogh painted with such expressive zeal in 1888–90, were compared by the artist, in his letters to his brother, to Egyptian obelisks. Surrealist Max Ernst, on the other hand, saw the forest as a murky haunt of fantasies, with works such as *Forest and Dove* (1927) emblems of the unconscious mind. By the first decade of this century, the motif of a black, fire-blasted tree had been used to denote the end of nature (and of civilisation) in Cormac McCarthy's *The Road* (2006). One of the earliest scenes in the film version of the novel features a tree falling with a menacing crash behind the two protagonists, a man and his son, as they make their way through a post-apocalyptic world. If the tree is an achetypical sign whose branches provide the perfect perch for countless concepts, not to mention an image rooted in some primitive, indelible part of human consciousness, it should come as no surprise that Havekost shows the tree like some wilting beast: your limbs would droop too if you had so many ideas foisted upon them.

The trees in *Gast* are at once grotesque and beautiful. Although the forms are organic, we never see the complete object—nor even a setting or landscape—just fragments: a torso, severed limbs. The insistent proximity of the trees, coupled with the ethereal afterglow of the camera flash, creates an atmosphere in which the viewer feels they are an invasive presence disturbing a nocturnal creature, to which they are nonetheless drawn. This tension

Lon Chaney in *The Phantom of the Opera* (1925)
© Bettmann/CORBIS

Eberhard Havekost, *Gast 9*, 2010

between the conflicting emotions of desire and fear that Havekost's work elicits evokes the aesthetics of horror movies, and recalls one of cinema's earliest moments of visceral terror: the unmasking scene in *The Phantom of the Opera* (1925). The phantom embodies a paradox: he desires, but his ugliness makes him repellent. He conceals his secret with a mask, which induces a level of desire in his prisoner, the singer Christine. When, finally, she lifts the mask to reveal his grisly visage, the phantom, played by Lon Chaney, turns from his organ and points his finger at the diva with a mix of accusation, horror and self-disgust, seeming both to attack her and recoil from her at the same time. Havekost's camera performs a similar unmasking: the light of the flash disturbs the tree, making it lurch in the night like a jilted monster, at once terrified and terrifying. It is this revelatory presence of the artist that transforms the tree from an everyday thing, or even from a specific tree in a specific place, into an object of attraction and repulsion.

Viewed together, the complete series of *Gast* becomes a proliferating forest, a regiment of clones. Havekost often depicts a single object or a set of objects from multiple viewpoints. His approach acknowledges that the visual world is infinite in its variety, and that almost any perspective could be framed to make a work of art. While this raises an important point about the equality of all things — and, by extension, about the validity of every perspective in a democracy — it leaves Havekost, as a figurative painter, with a problem: how does he choose his subject matter, and how much or how little information needs to be presented in order for an isolated set of visual phenomena to be termed a work of art? Havekost has explored this in earlier pieces, such as *Background* (2006) or *Regen 1* and *2* (2006), which show the same (or very similar) scene, based on photographs taken by the artist, from different viewpoints. *Background* features the jagged aftermath of a destroyed building, the scene also shot at night with a flash. *Regen 1* and *2*, a diptych, depicts some roadside trash, including a television, from slightly different angles. In both cases, Havekost introduces the importance of repetition, perspective and structure, and how these formal elements frame any interpretation of the work. More recently, in works such as *Normalität* (2009), the pictures have lost any immediately recognizable figurative element, playing instead with softly modulated surfaces that function on a level of visual pleasure, mystery and cadence. In *Triptychon* (2006), which also depicts a Weeping Nootka, we find this repetitive structure across three canvases, but the effect is worlds away from that of *Gast*. The pattern of interlocking greens and blacks is set against a flat blue background, giving the trees the desiccated appearance of a pressed flower. The limited palette and the slight variations in composition all contribute to the work's somewhat graphic appearance, as if the images were a series of design proposals for a logo. The painting has a reductive quality, offering hard but unarticulated details that question the minimum information required to signify a tree. The trees in

Gast, on the other hand, however ghostly they appear, have a depth and fleshiness to them; these trees are animated.

Havekost's *Gast* paintings present us with a paradox: as we try to approach their meaning, we find ourselves confronted by texture and rhythm instead. The images may not be immediately readable in the way Friedrich's *Winter Landscape* is, but nor do they represent an outpouring of the artist's mood or feelings, like the Abstract Expressionist paintings that they superficially resemble. The philosopher and art historian Richard Wollheim, in the last chapter of his book, *Painting as an Art*, distinguishes between textual metaphors in pictures and paintings that 'metaphorize' their content.[2] Friedrich's *Winter Landscape* contains textual metaphors: the viewer reads the trees as having clear religious significance. Havekost's trees do not resolve themselves into a clear textual meaning; they cannot be read as allegories. Rather, these trees participate viscerally in the ideas that they express. In Wollheim's terms, they 'metaphorize' their content — which is to say that they provoke emotions and fantasies in the viewer, and that the painting has a powerfully corporeal affect.

No matter how intensely the trees overwhelm our visual field with their unsettling, broken 'music' — the repetitive structure that is essential to the viewer being carried up and along with the rhythm of the series — most of us will look for other levels of meaning. But where? Looking at the vivid naturalism of Constable's Elm, the viewer might find a range of ideas about how the English in the early nineteenth century viewed nature: this is clearly a site of truth and beauty. Havekost, on the other hand, paints his urban evergreen as if it were draped in a leprous parchment. So subject matter can be important: the Weeping Nootka is an inherently beguiling thing, a weirdly expressive tree, whose qualities the artist has accentuated by depicting it eerily illuminated at night.

Havekost has created a forest for our era: a sad gang of apparitions haunted by metaphysics, unmasked at last by the contemporary painter. And, like the protagonist in a horror film, you may find yourself seduced by the monster, by the transfixing presence of each tree in this haunted forest. By repeating the motif from different viewpoints, moreover, Havekost strips the tree of its traditional referents, replacing a constellation of symbolic meanings with a rhythmic structure. For Havekost, this structure, this repetition, is content — everything else is just a story. Havekost has created an epistemology of looking, a model for how we perceive: *Gast* offers a dialogue and a dance.

1 Hölderlin, Friedrich (translated by Nick Hoff). *Odes and Elegies* (Middletown, CT: Wesleyan University Press 2008)

2 Wollheim, Richard. *Painting as an Art: A. W. Mellon Lectures in the Fine Arts v. 35*, Richard Wollheim (Princeton, NJ: Princeton University Press 1987)

Stand by, Interpretation Modus 1
2009
Oil on canvas
90 × 60 cm

Gast 1–2
2010
Oil on canvas
200 × 130 cm each

Stand by, Interpretation Modus 2
2009
Oil on canvas
90 × 60 cm

Gast 7–8
2010
Oil on canvas
200 × 130 cm each

Gast 9
2010
Oil on canvas
200 × 130 cm

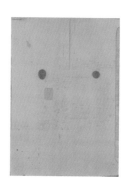

H2O
2009
Oil on canvas
130 × 90 cm

Normalität
2009
Oil on canvas (4 canvases)
90 × 60 cm each

Wand
2009
Oil on canvas
150 × 100 cm

Gast 3–6
2010
Oil on canvas
200×130 cm each

Distanz
2009
Oil on canvas
120×80 cm

Flatscreen
2009
Oil on canvas (6 canvases)
1 canvas: 150×100 cm
1 canvas: 110×70 cm
4 canvases: 90×60 cm

Geist
2009
Oil on canvas
90×60 cm

Fell
2008
Oil on canvas
160×100 cm

Zeitung 2
2009
Oil on canvas
150×100 cm

Goodbye, B09
2009
Oil on canvas
130×80 cm

Eberhard Havekost

Lives and works in Berlin
1991–1996 Hochschule für Bildende Künste Dresden
1967 Born in Dresden

Selected Solo Exhibitions

2010 Guest, White Cube, London
       Retina, Schirn Kunsthalle, Frankfurt
2009 Prints, Galerie Gebr. Lehmann, Berlin
       Le maniement nonchalant d'accessoires
       chers, Galerie Hussenot, Paris
       Style & Still, Anton Kern Gallery, New York
2008 Entrée, FRAC Auvergne, Clermont Ferrand,
       France
       The Unseen, Kunstparterre e.V., Munich
       Zensur 2, Galerie Gebr. Lehmann, Dresden
2007 Background, White Cube, London
       Zensur, Anton Kern Gallery, New York
2006 Harmony 2, Stedelijk Museum, Amsterdam
       Backstage, Galerie Gebr. Lehmann, Dresden
2005 Eberhard Havekost: Paintings from the
       Rubell Family Collection, Rubell Family
       Collection, Miami; American University
       Museum, Katzen Arts Center, Washington
       Art Gallery at Florida Gulf Coast University,
       Fort Myers and Tampa Museum of Art
       Harmonie, Kunstmuseum Wolfsburg,
       Germany
       Sonnenschutz, Roberts & Tilton Gallery,
       Los Angeles
2004 Circaware (with Olaf Holzapfel),
       Galerie Hussenot, Paris
       Brandung, Galerie Gebr. Lehmann, Dresden
       Graphik 1999–2004, Staatliche
       Kunstsammlungen, Dresden
       Project Room, Rubell Family Collection,
       Miami
       Marvel, Anton Kern Gallery, New York
2003 Eberhard Havekost,
       Lieu d'Art Contemporain, Sigean, France
       Eberhard Havekost, Centre d'art
       contemporain Georges Pompidou, Paris
       Dynamic UND, Inside the White Cube,
       London
       Beauty Walks a Razor's Edge,
       Galerie Gebr. Lehmann, Dresden
       McTREK CAMP 4 (with Hans-Peter
       Feldmann), Galerie Johnen+Schöttle,
       Cologne
2002 Square, Anton Kern Gallery, New York
2001 Driver, Museu de Arte Contemporanea de
       Serralves, Porto
       Eberhard Havekost / Martin Honert,
       Galerie Johnen+Schöttle, Cologne
       Dimmer, Galerie Gebr. Lehmann, Dresden
       J.F.B.-Hobby Industries (with Frank Nitsche),
       Galerie Onrust, Amsterdam
2000 Pressure-Pressure, Anton Kern Gallery,
       New York
       Mobile, Galerie Gebr. Lehmann, Dresden
1999 Kontakt, Galerie Gebr. Lehmann, Dresden
       Statements, Art Basel
       Flugplatz Reinsdorf, California
       (with Frank Nitsche), Kunsthalle Vierseithof,
       Luckenwalde, Germany

Druck Druck, Galerie für Zeitgenössische
Kunst, Leipzig
1998 Seestücke 2, Kunsthandlung Höhne,
       Cuxhaven, Germany
       Zoom, Anton Kern Gallery, New York
       Fenster-Fenster, Kunstmuseum Luzern,
       Switzerland
       Eberhard Havekost, Kommunale Galerie im
       Leinwandhaus, Frankfurt/Main
       Offene Gegend (with Thomas Scheibitz),
       Galerie Klaus-Peter Goebel, Stuttgart
       Geiz, Luxus (with Frank Nitsche),
       Kulturwissenschaftliches Institut, Essen
1997 Eberhard Havekost, Anton Kern Gallery,
       New York
       Frieren, Galerie Gebr. Lehmann, Dresden
       Abstecher I, Galerie Gebr. Lehmann, Dresden
       Forderkoje, Art Cologne, Cologne
1995 Wärme (with Thomas Scheibitz), Galerie
       Gebr. Lehmann, Dresden

Selected Group Exhibitions

2010 Celebration — Collection du Frac Auvergne,
       FRAC Auvergne, Clermont-Ferrand, France
2009 Zeigen. An Audio Tour through Berlin by
       Karin Sander, Temporäre Kunsthalle, Berlin
       Do They Love Their Children Too?,
       Milliken Gallery, Stockholm
       Listen to Your Eyes — Arbeiten aus der
       Sammlung Schmidt-Drenhaus, Galerie für
       Zeitgenössische Kunst, Leipzig
       60 Jahre 60 Werke — Kunst aus der
       Bundesrepublik Deutschland 1949–2009,
       Martin-Gropius-Bau, Berlin
       Ohne Uns!, Motorenhalle, Dresden
       Serralves 2009 — The Collection, Museu de
       Arte Contemporanea de Serralves, Porto
       La Rose Pourpre du Caire, Musée d'Art et
       d'Archéologie, Aurillac, France
       Gegen den Strich — 15 Jahre Sammlung,
       Kunstmuseum Wolfsburg, Germany
       Defiance & Melancholy — German Painting
       from the Dresden Albertinum / Galerie Neue
       Meister, Meilahti Art Museum, Helsinki
2008 The Painting of Modern Life,
       Castello di Rivoli, Turin
       Vom Schnee, Museum Kitzbühel, Austria
       Havekost, Lucander, Pflumm, Milliken
       Gallery, Stockholm
       Macrocosm, Roberts and Tilton,
       Los Angeles
       Konstellationen IV, Städel Museum,
       Frankfurt/Main
       Paradies und Zurueck, Sammlung Rheingold
       auf Schloss Dyck, Juechen, Germany
       Comme des Bêtes, Musée Cantonal des
       Beaux-Arts, Lausanne, Switzerland

Living Landscapes — A Journey Through German Art, National Art Museum, Beijing

2007   *Visite — Von Gerhard Richter bis Rebecca Horn — Werke aus der Sammlung Zeitgenössischer Kunst der BRD*, Palais des Beaux-Arts, Brussels

Deutsche und Amerikanische Malerei in der Sammlung Frieder Burda, Museum Frieder Burda, Baden-Baden, Germany

I can only see things when I move — Positionen Zeitgenössischer Kunst auf Papier, Ausstellung des Kupferstich-Kabinetts, Residenzschloss, Dresden

Painting Now!, Kunsthal Rotterdam

The Evil — Pop & Politik, Galerie Gebr. Lehmann, Dresden

Imagination Becomes Reality, Sammlung Goetz, Munich and ZMK Museum of Contemporary Art Karlsruhe, Germany

The Painting of Modern Life, Hayward Gallery, London

A Tribute — 35 Years of the Essl Collection, Essl Museum, Klosterneuburg, Austria

Six Feet Under, Deutsches Hygiene-Museum, Dresden

Gesellschaftsbilder — Zeitgenössische Malerei, Kunstverein Hamburg

2006   *Life After Death — New Leipzig Painting from the Rubell Family Collection*, American University Museum, Katzen Arts Center, Washington

Von Beuys bis Havekost, Sammlung Marx at Hamburger Bahnhof, Berlin

Below the Surface, Stedelijk Museum, Amsterdam

Implosion, Anton Kern Gallery, New York

Neue Malerei, Museum Frieder Burda, Baden-Baden, Germany

Images in Painting, Museu de Arte Contemporanea de Serralves, Porto

The Triumph of Painting, Leeds City Art Gallery

Heile Welt, Kupferstich-Kabinett, Staatliche Kunstsammlungen Dresden

The Trace of a Trace, Perry Rubenstein Gallery, New York

Constructing New Berlin, Phoenix Art Museum, Arizona

Painting S(e)oul, Kukje Gallery, Seoul

Construction, Ratio and Sense, Galerist Istanbul

The Other Side 2, Tony Shafrazi Gallery, New York

The Other Side, Tony Shafrazi Gallery, New York

Anstoss Berlin — Kunst Macht Welt, Haus am Waldsee, Berlin

Zurück zur Figur, Hypo-Kunsthalle, Munich

Material Gestures, Tate Modern, London

Verstehen Braucht Kontext II, Malkasten, Düsseldorf

Auch das Unnatürlichste ist die Natur, Galerie Michael Neff, Frankfurt/Main

Wintersport, Kunstforum Montafon, Schruns, Austria

Wrestle, Hessel Museum of Art, Annandale on Hudson, New York

Kulturinvest, Oktogon der HfBK, Dresden

2005   *Imagination Becomes Reality — Painting Surface Space*, Sammlung Goetz, Munich

Trials and Terrors, Museum of Contemporary Art Chicago

Styles und Stile, Sofia Art Gallery

Some Trees, Galerie Neue Meister, Dresden

Private View 1980-2000 — Collection Pierre Huber, Musée Cantonal des Beaux-Arts, Lausanne, Switzerland

Greater than the Sum, University Gallery of Florida, Gainesville, Florida

Do It Yourself, Sammlung Marx at Hamburger Bahnhof, Berlin

Generation X, Kunstmuseum Wolfsburg

Das Schillern, Goethe Institut, Rotterdam

Die Eröffnung — 200 Jahre Kunst, Städtische Galerie Dresden

Urbane Realitäten — Fokus Istanbul, Martin-Gropius-Bau, Berlin

La Nouvelle Peinture Allemande, Carré d'Art, Nîmes, France

Arte Contemporáneo, Museo Municipal de Málaga

36×27×10, White Cube, London and Palast der Republik, Berlin

2004   *Support — The Neue Galerie as a Collection — 1950 — Today*, Neue Galerie Graz, Austria

Eröffnungsausstellung Sammlung Frieder Burda, Museum Frieder Burda and Staatliche Kunsthalle, Baden-Baden, Germany

Landschafts-Paraphrasen, Städtische Galerie Gladbeck, Germany

Eye of the Needle, Roberts & Tilton Gallery, Los Angeles

Artists' Favourites (Act II), Institute of Contemporary Arts, London

Direct Painting, Kunsthalle Mannheim, Germany

Sammlung Plum, Museum Kurhaus Kleve, Germany

Weltsichten, Kupferstich-Kabinett, Dresden

Fehlfarben, Residenzschloss and Gläserne Manufaktur, Dresden

Nouvelles Collections, Centre PasquArt, Biel, Switzerland

Pixels, Stellan Holm Gallery, New York

Heißkalt — Sammlung Scharpff, Staatsgalerie Stuttgart

94–04 Zehn Jahre Gesellschaft für Moderne Kunst in Dresden, Galerie Neue Meister, Dresden

Die Falle Wirklichkeit, Malkasten, Dusseldorf

Happy Birthday — Werke der Sammlung, Kunstmuseum Wolfsburg, Germany

Treasure Island, Kunstmuseum Wolfsburg,
Germany
realityREAL, Galerie Gebr. Lehmann, Dresden
2003 *Painting Pictures*, Kunstmuseum Wolfsburg,
Germany
Prague Biennale 1, National Gallery, Prague
Interview with Painting, Fondazione
Bevilacqua La Masa, Venice
deutschemalereizweitausenddrei, Frankfurter
Kunstverein, Frankfurt/Main
In Your Face, Frahm Ltd, London
Berlin-Moskau 1950–2000,
Martin-Gropius-Bau, Berlin
Special Edition, Galerie Suzanne Tarasieve,
Paris
Heißkalt — Sammlung Scharpff,
Hamburger Kunsthalle
Karl Schmidt-Rottluff Stipendium,
Kunsthalle Düsseldorf
Hands Up Baby Hands Up!, Oldenburger
Kunstverein, Oldenburg, Germany
2002 *Five Years — Rue Louise Weiss*, Galerie
Jennifer Flay, Paris
*Galerie Gebr. Lehmann bei Galerie Michael
Neff* featuring Galerie Gebr. Lehmann,
Frankfurt/Main
Sub-Urban, Loop, Berlin
Wunschbilder, Museum der bildenden
Künste, Leipzig
Whisper, Galerie Aurel Scheibler, Cologne
1000 und 86, Kupferstich-Kabinett,
Staatliche Kunstsammlungen Dresden
2001 *Painting at the Edge of the World*,
Walker Art Center, Minneapolis
The Way I See it, Galerie Jennifer Flay, Paris
Schock Sensor, AR/GE Galleria Museo,
Bolzano, Italy
Erworben, Kunstfonds des Freistaates
Sachsen, Dresdner Schloss,
Georgenbau, Dresden
Musterkarte — Modelos de Pintura, Centro
Cultural Conde Duque, Madrid
Das gute Leben, Galerie Gebr. Lehmann,
Dresden
Freunde Schenken Kunst, Museis Saxonicis
Usui Albertinum, Dresden
Frisch gerahmt, Bonner Kunstverein, Bonn
I Love NY, Anton Kern Gallery, New York
Schock Sensor 2,
Städtische Galerie Gladbeck, Germany
2000 *Gut aufgelegt, 75 Jahre Griffelkunst-
Vereinigung*, Kunsthaus, Hamburg
Extra Ordinary, James Cohan Gallery,
New York
Der abgelenkte Blick, Helmhaus Zürich
Mixing Memory and Desire, Neues
Kunstmuseum, Luzern, Switzerland
Europa Differenti Prospettive Nella Pittura,
Museo Michetti, Francavilla al Mare, Italy
*Die Andauernden Städte — Urbane
Situationen*, Galerie im Taxispalais,
Innsbruck, Austria

*Sausage & Frankfurters: Recent British
and German Paintings from the Ophiuchus
Collection*, Ophiuchus Collection, Hydra,
Greece
Herbstsalon 2000, Neuer Sächsischer
Kunstverein, Dresden
25 Jahre Karl Schmidt-Rottluff Stipendium,
Oktogon der HfBK, Dresden
Goldener — Der Springer — Das kalte Herz,
White Cube, London
*Wahre Wunder — Sammler & Sammlungen
im Rheinland*, Josef Haubrich-Kunsthalle,
Cologne
Die Künstlerstiftung, Kunsthalle Düsseldorf
1999 *Zauber Haft*, Am Brauhaus 5, Dresden
Umzug, Galerie Gebr. Lehmann, Dresden
Mietfrei, Galerie Gebr. Lehmann, Dresden
Wege der Deutschen 1949–99,
Martin-Gropus-Bau, Berlin
In Augenhöhe, Neuer Berliner Kunstverein,
Berlin
Malerei, INIT — Kunsthalle, Berlin
Pictures of Pictures, Norwich Gallery, UK
Norwich School of Art and Design and
Arnolfini Gallery, Bristol, UK
Bilder aus Städten, Dresdner Bank,
Frankfurt/Main
*Persuasion — Tales of Commerce and the
Avant Garde*, University at Buffalo Art
Gallery, New York
1998 *Gegenstand*, Galerie Sfeir-Semler, Kiel,
Germany
Gallery by Night, Studio Gallery, Budapest
Zwei Stufen, Künstlerhaus Schloss
Wiepersdorf, Germany
ACHSE 3zu01, Hochschule für Bildende
Künste, Dresden
Go East, Wollongong City Gallery, Sydney
College of the Arts Gallery
Sichtverhältnisse Madrid — Berlin, Centro
Cultural del Conde Duque, Madrid and
Künstlerhaus Bethanien, Berlin
Dorothea von Stetten-Kunstpreis,
Kunstmuseum Bonn
1997 *Fotogelb*, Galerie Gebr. Lehmann, Dresden
Artist in Residence, Neue Galerie Graz,
Austria
Vier/VI, Leonhardi-Museum, Dresden
1996 *Neu im Kabinett*, Staatliche
Kunstsammlungen, Dresden
Fin, Kurfürstenpassage Dresden
1995 *Fantastic-Elastic*, Kunst-Konsum, Dresden

Selected Solo Exhibition Catalogues
and Artist's Books

Häusler, Heide and Max Hollein (eds.), *Retina* (Walther Koenig, Cologne 2010)

Vergne, Jean-Charles (ed.), *Entrée* (FRAC Auvergne, Clermont-Ferrand, France 2008)

Wagner, Thomas, *Eberhard Havekost: Künstler — Kritisches Lexikon der Gegenwartskunst* (Weltkunstverlag, Munich 2008)

Heiner, Bastian and Eberhard Havekost, *Benutzeroberfläche/User Interface* (Schirmer/Mosel Verlag, Munich 2007)

Herbert, Martin, *Eberhard Havekost: Background* (White Cube, London 2007)

Coetzee, Mark, Meghan Dailey and Ulrich Loock, *Eberhard Havekost 1996–2006: Paintings From The Rubell Family Collection* (Rubell Family Collection, Miami 2006)

Eberhard Havekost: Harmonie: Bilder/Paintings: 2000–05 (Hatje Cantz, Ostfildern-Ruit and Kunstmuseum Wolfsburg, 2005); texts by Thomas Kühler, Annelie Lütgens, Ludwig Seyfarth and Suzanne Kühler

Eberhard Havekost: Graphik 1999–2004 (Walther Koenig, Cologne 2004); texts by Martin Roth, Rainer Stange, Tobias Burg and Hans-Ulrich Lehmann,

Guimaraes, Sandra (ed.), *Eberhard Havekost: Driver* (Museu de Arte Contemporanea Serralves, Porto 2001)

Ackermann, Andreas, *Geiz, Luxus* (Kulturwissenschaftliches Institut, Essen 1999)

Werner, Klaus, Bernhard Schwenk and Fabrice Hergott, *Druck: Eberhard Havekost* (Ostdeutsche Sparkassenstiftung im Freistaat Sachsen, Leipzig 1999)

Klemp, Klaus and Christoph Tannert, *Eberhard Havekost* (Kommunale Galerie im Leinwandhaus, Frankfurt and Verlag der Kunst, Dresden 1998)

Loock, Ulrich, *Eberhard Havekost: Fenster* (Kunstmuseum Luzern, Switzerland 1998)

Hegewisch, Katharina, *Seestücke: Eberhard Havekost* (Hypo-Bank, Rostock, Germany 1997)

Wärme: Eberhard Havekost und Thomas Scheibitz (Galerie Gebr. Lehmann, Dresden 1995)